THE VALUE OF DEDICATION

The Story of Albert Schweitzer

VALUE COMMUNICATIONS, INC.
PUBLISHERS
LA JOLLA, CALIFORNIA

THE
VALUE
OF
DEDICATION

The Story of
Albert Schweitzer

BY SPENCER JOHNSON, M.D.

THE DANBURY PRESS

The Value of Dedication is part of the ValueTales series.

The Value of Dedication text copyright © 1979 by Spencer
Johnson, M.D. Illustrations copyright © 1979 by Value
Communications, Inc.

First Edition
Manufactured in the United States of America
For information write to: ValueTales, P.O. Box 1012
La Jolla, CA 92038

Library of Congress Cataloging in Publication Data

Johnson, Spencer.
    The value of dedication.

    (ValueTales)
    SUMMARY: Presents a biography of Albert Schweitzer
who based his philosophy on what he called "reverence for
life" and dedicated his life to serving humanity.
    1.   Schweitzer, Albert, 1875-1965—Juvenile literature.
2.   Missionaries, Medical—Gabon—Biography—Juvenile
literature.   3.   Theologians—Europe—Biography—
Juvenile literature.   4.   Musicians—Europe—Biography—
Juvenile literature.   5.   Altruism—Juvenile literature.
[1.   Schweitzer, Albert, 1875-1965.   2.   Missionaries.
3.   Theologians.   4.   Musicians.   5.   Altruism]I.   Title.
CT1018.S45J63   266'.025'0924 [B] [92]   79-21805

ISBN 0-916392-44-9

This tale is about a man who was very dedicated to his fellowman, Albert Schweitzer. The story that follows is based on events in his life. More historical facts about Albert Schweitzer can be found on page 63.

Once upon a time...

not so very long ago, a young student named Albert Schweitzer was on his way home from the university for his spring vacation.

"How beautiful it is here!" he said to himself when he arrived in the tiny village in Alsace where his father was the minister. He could smell lilacs in bloom, and he knew that the apple orchards nearby were soft with blossoms.

Albert hurried as fast as his legs would carry him to the house where his parents lived. He hugged his mother and shook hands with his father. Then he went upstairs to put his things in his own small, sunny bedroom under the eaves.

Albert sat up late that night talking with his parents, so he slept late the next morning. When he woke, the sun was coming through the window and the bees were buzzing among the flowers in his mother's garden.

Albert felt happy, so happy that he could not possibly lie in bed. He got up and threw on his clothes, and he went out to walk in the woods near the village.

8

He had not gone far before he heard a pitiful whimpering sound.
It came from the underbrush near the path.

"Some little animal is hurt," said Albert. He stooped to push aside
a bramble, and he saw that a young fox was caught in a snare.

"Well now," said Albert, "you surely don't belong in a trap on
such a fine spring morning."

Albert freed the fox, and he watched it scamper off into the forest.

"Poor little creature," said Albert. "His life is as precious to him as mine is to me. And why not? All life is precious."

Albert then sat down on a fallen log and thought about life. He thought especially about his own life, and how good it was. He had a fine family, and they loved him. He was strong and healthy. He was a talented musician and a brilliant student.

"I have been given so many gifts," said Albert to himself. "How can I take them for granted? I must share them."

Albert wondered then just how he would share his gifts. "I am twenty-one now," he said, after a bit. "I will give myself nine years. During that nine years, I will develop all of my talents. Then, when I am thirty, I will dedicate myself to serving other people."

Albert looked up. He thought for a moment that the fox was still there, watching from beneath the brambles. "What do you think, Reynard?" he said. "Isn't that a good plan?"

"It is the sort of plan a young man makes on a lovely spring day," said the fox. "By the time you are thirty, you will have forgotten it. You will be doing the things all men do. You will be wearing fine clothes and making money and wondering why you aren't more famous."

Albert laughed. He knew that the fox really wasn't talking to him. He knew he was listening to his own inner self. It was warning him to be steadfast. He decided then that perhaps he should remember the fox always, so that he could never forget his decision.

"We shall see, Reynard," he said.

"Why do you call me that?" asked the fox.

"Because in the fables the fox is always called Reynard," said Albert. "Now you come along with me, and when I want to talk to someone about my plan, I will talk to you. I won't tell anyone else. It will be a secret."

"It had better be a secret," said the fox. "If your parents could hear you now, they'd send for the doctor to see if you had caught some strange disease."

Albert laughed again. Then he went home and he said not a word to his parents about his decision. And in the nine years that followed that bright spring morning, Albert did many things that most young men never do.

He became a famous organist and gave concerts in the great churches where there were wonderful old organs.

He became a minister like his father, and every Sunday he conducted services in a church in Strasbourg.

14

He wrote a book about organs and a book about the great composer, Johann Sebastian Bach. He wrote other books about theology and philosophy. He was even the principal of a college.

"Albert Schweitzer is a genius," people said. "How does he find time to do all the things he does? Doesn't he ever sleep?"

"Not a great deal, I'm afraid," Reynard always replied. The fox would yawn when he said this, and no one would pay any attention. Perhaps this was because no one but Albert ever saw Reynard.

Fortunately Albert was very strong. He could get along without much sleep. But when he was in his mid-twenties, something happened that caused him to worry and wonder.

Do you know what it was?

It was a meeting with a girl. Her name was Helene, and she was very pretty, with dark eyes and dark hair. For the first time Albert wanted to talk with someone besides Reynard about his plans. He wanted to talk with Helene.

"But will she understand?" he asked.

Reynard chuckled. "No," he said. "She'll think that you're mad and she'll probably never bother with you again."

"I'm afraid I can't help that," said Albert. "I have to tell her."

But before Albert could decide what to say about his decision to dedicate his life to others, he learned a most astonishing thing about Helene.

"I'm very fortunate," she said one day. "I have good health and a good family, and I'm not stupid. I've decided that I can't take these things for granted. I have to share them. So, when I'm twenty-five, I'm going to dedicate myself to serving other people. I'm going to study nursing."

Albert felt like turning handsprings. He felt like singing. He also felt that perhaps he might ask Helene to marry him, and in time he did just that.

But before Helene and Albert could be married, Albert had some more decisions to make and some more work to do. He was twenty-nine when he knew at last how he would serve humanity.

18

"I want to go to the Congo," he told Helene. "I've been reading about the people there. They suffer greatly from tropical diseases. I want to become a doctor so that I can treat their illnesses."

"A doctor?" cried Helene. "But that will mean spending another six or seven years as a medical student!"

It seemed too much even for Helene to understand. But she saw that Albert was determined, and she did not try to persuade him to do things in an easier way. So Albert wrote to his parents and to his close friends. He told them he would enter Strasbourg University as a medical student.

"You've lost your mind!" said his friends.

"I don't believe so," said Albert. Then he moved his things out of the bright, cheery rooms that had been his when he was principal of a college. He moved into shabby little rooms high up in an attic. And he set to work.

Soon he knew about drab, drafty laboratories and long, dull lectures. He spent hours studying anatomy and chemistry. When he grew too weary, he would slip into a church near the university and play the organ. It always refreshed him.

Soon he was giving concerts again and writing more books. Still, he studied as hard as any student in the university.

"Sometimes I'm sorry I ever met you," Reynard would say to him. "You make me feel like a lazy fox."

"You *are* a lazy fox," Albert answered, "and I am a sturdy peasant. I'm strong as a horse. A little extra work will never hurt me."

The extra work didn't hurt Albert. Indeed, it seemed to make him stronger.

"How odd," said one of his professors. "The more he does, the more he seems able to do."

"That's because he's so dedicated," said another man. "He puts all of his heart—all of his energy—into his work and his music. He doesn't do anything halfway, so he can do a great deal."

Albert passed his examinations in 1911, and for a year he was an intern. Then he presented himself to the Paris Missionary Society.

"I want to go to Africa," he said, "and I need your help. I'm a doctor. Send me to a place where there's a hospital and I'll take no salary. I have written many books, and I can live off the money that comes to me from the publishers of those books."

"I don't think they're going to be able to turn down an offer like that," said Reynard the fox.

Reynard was quite right. The members of the Missionary Society accepted Albert's offer. He hurried to Strasbourg to tell Helene the good news.

"They will send me to a place called Lambaréné," he said. He opened a map he had brought so that Helene could see where it was—on a river called the Ogowe in a country named Gabon. It was on the west coast of Africa.

"It's almost at the equator," said Helene. "It will be terribly hot there."

"Do you think you can put up with it?" asked Albert. "And are you sure you can put up with *me* way out there in Africa? There won't be other Europeans around."

"Of course I can put up with you," said Helene. "It's what I have wanted ever since I met you."

So Albert and Helene were married. Within a few months they were aboard a steamer bound for Africa.

Albert and Helene had crates and bales and boxes filled with medicines and supplies for their hospital. In one really huge crate was a special piano the Paris Bach Society had given to Albert. It was lined with lead so that the dampness of the jungle would not harm it.

At the mouth of the Ogowe River there was a town named Cape Lopez. When their steamer docked there, Albert and Helene—and all of their boxes and bales and crates—were put aboard a smaller boat. It was a little river steamer that would take them almost to their destination at Lambaréné.

"The last few miles we will travel by canoe," said Albert. He was watching the hippos in the river.

"I don't think I'm going to like that," said Reynard.

The fox had come along with Albert and Helene, and now he did not look like a happy, frisky young fox. He looked like a frightened fox. He had seen the dark forests all along the shores of the river. He had glimpsed the wild animals that moved in the twilight under the trees.

When they were 250 miles from Cape Lopez, they left the river steamer and got into the canoes that had come to meet them.

"We will send your supplies after you as soon as we get more canoes and more men to row," promised the captain of the river steamer. "As for your piano—well, we will do the best we can. It will not be easy. It weighs three tons!"

"If we must live in the forest without music, that is what we will do," said Albert. Then he and Helene went on in the dugouts.

"I have become a civilized fox," said Reynard. "I am not sure I approve of all this."

Albert paid no attention. He was eager now. He could not wait to see the hospital where he would work to help the suffering people of Africa. At last, after what seemed an eternity, his canoe rounded a bend in the river. A tall man in the prow pointed ahead. "That is Lambaréné," he said.

What do you suppose Albert saw?

He saw a clearing on the riverbank. There were a few tumbledown shacks, and the forest seemed to press in close to them as if it would gobble them up.

"Is that my hospital?" cried Albert. He was stunned.

"I knew it would not be easy," said Helene, "but I had hoped it would not be *this* hard!"

That night Albert and Helene slept in a little house in the clearing. It was built on stilts so that, when the river rose, it would not be swept away.

"Very sensible!" said Reynard. He looked at the little creatures that scuttled on the floor, and he wrinkled his nose. "Now if only they had found a way to keep out the spiders and the cockroaches and the centipedes."

Albert sighed. "You're right," he told Reynard. "I don't care at all for the centipedes. But don't think I'm giving up. I'm going to stay right here. And because there really *isn't* a hospital, I'm going to build one!"

31

The next day Albert and Helene set to work. There was an old chicken house in the clearing, and they decided that this would be their clinic. They swept the floor clean and whitewashed the walls. Then Albert built shelves so that he would have a place to put his medicines.

"Tidy enough," said Reynard, "but not much like the laboratories at Strasbourg, is it?"

Albert shook his head. "Not much like the hospital where I was an intern, either. Never mind. Until we can build something better, it will have to do."

"I thought you'd say that," declared the fox. "That's what a dedicated man would say. And you seem to have finished it just in time."

"In time for what?" asked Albert.

"Come and look," said Reynard.

The fox trotted to the door of the chicken house. Albert followed him and looked out onto the river.

There were canoes—dozens of canoes. In each canoe there were several people.

"The word seems to have spread that there's a doctor at Lambaréné," said Reynard. "They have come to be treated."

"But . . . but there are so many!" cried Albert, as the first of the sick people was helped forward by his friends.

"You did not want to practice medicine all by yourself, did you?" asked the fox.

Albert used a camp bed for an operating table. Helene assisted him as he worked.

Many of the patients had injured themselves working in the mahogany forests, cutting trees and carrying logs. Some had malaria. Some had dysentery. Some had sleeping sickness, which was spread by the bite of a tsetse fly. Unless Albert could help them, the victims would slip into a coma and never wake again.

"So much to do," said Albert, after his first day in the
makeshift hospital.

"You know what your professors used to say about you,"
Reynard reminded him. "The more you do, the more you can do,
because you put your heart into it."

Just then a tall, handsome native came up to Albert. "The doctor
wants help?" asked the man. He spoke in French.

"My name is Joseph," said the man. "Joseph Azoawami. If you like, I will be assistant to you. I am a strong man and I know many things."

Albert smiled. "What is it that you know, Joseph?" he asked.

"I know how to speak English and French," said Joseph. "Also, I can speak eight different African languages. And if you tell me a thing, I will not forget it again."

"Very well," said Albert. "We shall see what sort of assistant you will make."

The tall man grinned. "I will come in the morning," he promised. "I will show you. You will be very happy."

He turned and went away across the clearing. Reynard the fox came and leaned against Albert's leg. "I have a feeling this is the beginning of a long friendship," he said.

Reynard was right, as he often proved to be. Joseph knew many things that were useful to Albert and Helene.

He had been a cook, so he knew some anatomy. Often he said such things as, "This man has a pain in his leg of mutton." Then Albert would imagine how a leg of mutton looked, and he would know just where the pain must be.

Joseph could not read, but he knew from the shape of the writing on a medicine bottle what was inside. Soon he had learned exactly what to give the patients who came to Albert's hospital.

He learned how to help during operations, too. Helene would be ready with the ether when a patient was brought in for surgery. Joseph stood by. He was very clean and very scrubbed and very proud. He wore rubber gloves and handed instruments to Albert.

In time, all of Albert's supplies came. They were brought by huge canoes made from the trunks of giant trees. Even the three-ton piano came and was carried into Albert's little house. When Albert was tired—and he often was—he would sit at the instrument and play.

"You used to do that when you were wearying of studying medicine," said Reynard.

"I am even more weary now," said Albert. "I am sad. I feel that there is a heavy weight on my heart. Reynard, there is so much disease and pain here, and pain is a more terrible thing even than death."

"You don't need to stay," Reynard reminded him. "You can go home again. No one would blame you."

"I cannot go home again," said Albert. "I must help these people. They are my brothers. Besides, what is my life worth if I don't dedicate it to something that is magnificent and difficult? What sort of person can be merely comfortable?"

"Not you, I'm sure!" said Reynard.

Albert played with more spirit then, and he struck great, crashing, wonderful chords. Then he got up and went out to work some more. It was the way it had been at medical school. The more he did, the more he could do.

In a few months there were more buildings in the hospital clearing. One was made with corrugated iron walls and roof. It took the place of the ramshackle little chicken house. There was a storehouse for medical supplies. There were huts, too, for the patients to stay in. Until these were built, Albert's patients had been camping out under the trees.

"I think we have a very fine hospital," said Joseph proudly. "I think in all of Africa there are not many hospitals so fine as this. I think that the first assistant to the doctor at Lambaréné should have a wife."

"A fine idea, Joseph," said Albert. "Why don't you have a wife?"

"Because I have not saved enough money yet to buy one," said Joseph.

45

Albert was not surprised. He knew that in Gabon at that time a man had to purchase a wife if he wanted one. But he stared at Joseph's feet.

"Joseph, you are wearing a pair of shiny new boots," he said. "Why did you spend money for the boots when the first assistant to the doctor at Lambaréné needs a wife?"

"Because," answered Joseph, "it is only right for the first assistant to the doctor at Lambaréné to have boots."

Then Joseph went off to meet the river steamer to see whether any new supplies had come for the hospital.

Reynard chuckled. "He is right, you know," he said. "The doctor's assistant should have shiny boots. I think perhaps the doctor's assistant should have so many things that he will never save enough for a wife."

Albert nodded, and he did not think of it again until he saw Joseph coming back from the river. Joseph was running, and he was being most careless about his elegant, shiny boots.

"Doctor! Doctor! A terrible thing has happened!" he cried. "The steamer captain brought the news," said Joseph. "Far away in Europe there is a war."

47

Albert felt a coldness in his heart. He had been afraid of this. The year was 1914, and there were bad feelings between the German and the French. And now, with the two countries at war, he and Helene were enemy aliens. They were Germans in French territory.

Helene came from the house. She looked terribly worried. "What will happen?" she said.

"Who knows?" Albert's face was stern. "They may close the hospital and send us away. How will I ever explain it to the patients? How can I tell them about the madness that makes men kill each other in a war."

Albert's shoulders were bent as if he carried a heavy burden. For there, leading his difficult, dedicated life in Africa, he had come to believe that life was holy. He felt that every man was part of this holiness. He believed that each of his patients was a part of his own life, and that even animals and insects and plants and trees were sacred because they were alive.

Soon the hospital at Lambaréné was closed. The patients were sent home. Only Joseph remained to guard the medicines.

Albert and Helene were transported back to France. It was to be seven long years before Albert saw the hospital at Lambaréné again.

For a while Albert and Helene stayed in Bordeaux, where they were kept under guard. Then they were moved to a monastery in the Pyrenees. There were many people there who had been caught in the confusion of the war and who could not get to their homes again.

"There are scholars here, Albert," said Reynard. Of course the fox had come along to the monastery. He went everywhere with Albert, and his bright eyes missed nothing. "They have come from all over the world," the fox went on. "A dedicated man might learn a lot from them."

What do you think Albert did when he heard that?

51

He began talking with the learned people. He became excited about ideas. He argued about theology and philosophy.

"You're acting like a young student again," said Reynard.

"I know!" cried Albert. "It feels good to act like a young student!"

Then Albert began to write again, and to practice his music. When he had no organ or piano, he fingered pieces on a tabletop or the top of a trunk. He could always hear the music in his head.

The Schweitzers went home to Germany in 1918. Soon after the war ended, Helene presented Albert with a wonderful gift—a lovely little daughter born on Albert's forty-fourth birthday.

"Now will you stay in Europe?" asked Reynard. "Surely you won't take that beautiful baby to Lambaréné. You know it isn't healthy there for Europeans—or for anyone!"

"I won't take her," Albert decided, "but as soon as I can raise some money for supplies and equipment and perhaps more buildings, I will go myself. I must. The people there are my people, aren't they?"

So Albert went back to Africa, and Helene stayed with the baby in Strasbourg.

When Albert reached Lambaréné, he found that the corrugated iron building was all that remained of his hospital. Even that had no roof.

"The jungle crept in," said Joseph. "It ate up the huts and the storehouse. That is what happens here."

"We must build again," said Albert, and he began.

Soon Albert had a hospital again, and he had another doctor to help him. The second doctor arrived just in time, for there was an outbreak of dysentery in the area. Albert worked long and hard, but many people died. At last Albert became terribly discouraged.

"Why can't they listen?" he cried. "I tell them not to drink the river water. It's polluted and it makes them sick. Oh, what a blockhead I was to come out here!"

"Yes, doctor," said Joseph. "Here on earth you are truly a blockhead. But I think that in heaven you are no blockhead."

Albert took heart when Joseph said this, and he felt more cheerful. In time the dysentery epidemic passed. But there were always problems and there was never enough room.

"We need a bigger hospital," Albert said to Reynard, "and I think I know just where it should be."

Albert took a motor launch and cruised up the river. Two miles beyond his old hospital he came to a point of land where two hundred acres had been cleared. "Isn't that beautiful!" Albert exclaimed to Reynard.

"The jungle will creep in again," warned Reynard. "In the rainy season, the river will rise."

"We will build everything on piles, high above the level of the river," said Albert. "We will plant orchards to grow fruit, and we will sow grain in the space that is left."

Reynard sighed. "Dedication is a very fine thing, I suppose," said he, "but it surely isn't a bit restful."

"We can rest when we're dead, Reynard," laughed Albert. "Right now we have work to do!"

All through that winter the patients who were well enough to work labored for the new hospital. So did their friends who came from the villages up and down the river. Albert paid them in food and in presents—spoons and cooking pots and blankets and mosquito netting.

When the hospital was finished, there was a great celebration on the river. Motorboats came from far and near. They chugged back and forth between the new hospital and the old one, moving supplies and equipment. People who didn't have motorboats helped with dugouts. There were streamers and banners. There were shouts and songs.

"Isn't it grand?" said Albert. He was very happy.

"Yes, it is," said Reynard. He looked at the forty huts for the patients and at the larger buildings raised up on pilings. The new Lambaréné hospital could house six or seven hundred people. "Many villages aren't so big," said the fox.

The years passed, and war came to Europe again. But this time Albert was able to remain at Lambaréné, and Helene came to join him. He worked hard all those years, and he always found time to write about life—about his reverence for life and his dedication to it.

"Aren't you weary?" said Reynard once. "Why don't you rest!"

"Because my humanity is like money," said Albert. "If I keep it in a jar on a shelf, it can do nothing. But if I spend it on others, who knows what can happen?"

What did happen to Albert was that his dedication to the people at Lambaréné—and to all living things—became known the world over. He was honored by governments and universities and learned societies. Queen Elizabeth presented him with the Order of Merit, and in 1952 an emissary came from Stockholm to ask if he would accept the Nobel Peace Prize.

Albert accepted, of course. The prize was $33,000, and he could use the money to build a new building at Lambaréné.

Not everyone can become a doctor and go to Africa like Albert Schweitzer, but there will always be work dedicated people can do. That is one thing Albert taught the world. It's something you might want to think about.

Sometimes dedication produces grand results. Hospitals are built. Diseases are cured. But dedication can be quite simple. Every day dedicated people are kinder and more helpful to those around them.

Only you can decide whether dedication to something outside yourself can give your life great meaning, and can make you a better, more complete person . . . just like our good friend Albert Schweitzer.

The End

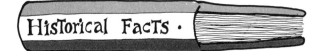

Historical Facts ·

Albert Schweitzer was born on January 14, 1875, in Alsace, which at that time belonged to Germany. As an infant he was so frail that his mother was almost ashamed to let him be seen by friends and neighbors in the little town of Günsbach, where the Schweitzers made their home. She determined that he would grow to be well and strong, and she took such good care of him that by the time he was two he was a sturdy, healthy toddler. For all of his life after that, he would be capable of remarkable and prolonged exertion.

Albert was the son of a minister, and he grew up in a household where theology was an everyday concern and where music was also taken for granted. His father started giving him piano lessons before he was old enough to go to school. When his legs were long enough to reach the pedals on the organ in the village church, he persuaded the organist there to show him how to use the stops. He did so well that, when he was only nine, the organist allowed him to play for the morning services.

In October of 1893, Albert became a student at the University of Strasbourg. It was during a short vacation from the university that Albert decided that he would spend his time until he became thirty absorbing the things of the mind that he loved and that thereafter he would devote his life to serving mankind. He never wavered from this decision, and he was especially fortunate when he met Helene Bresslau, the daughter of a famous Strasbourg historian. She had also felt the call to dedicate her life to suffering humanity. When Albert announced that he would become a doctor and go to Africa, Helene was happy to share his mission with him.

In 1912, Albert obtained his doctorate in medicine from the University of Strasbourg. Soon after he went out to Lambaréné, Gabon, in French Equatorial Africa.

The hospital Albert built at Lambaréné eventually became famous throughout the world, and many people sent money to support it, but in the beginning Albert had to struggle. He was not in Africa long before World War I broke out, and he

ALBERT SCHWEITZER
1875–1965

and Helene were returned to France, where they were interned as enemy aliens in a monastery in the Pyrenees Mountains. Seven years later he returned to Africa to find his hospital a ruin. He rebuilt and enlarged it, and for the rest of his life he made frequent trips back to Europe to lecture and give concerts so that he could raise money to support his work at Lambaréné.

Albert Schweitzer was not only a doctor: he was a philosopher, a theologian, and a musicologist. He is famed in musical circles as the editor of Bach's organ music and the author of a biography of the great composer. His philosophical writings brought him the respect of the academic world. But it was his humanitarian efforts in Africa that earned him world fame and won for him the Nobel Peace Prize. The books he wrote about his African experiences are *On the Edge of the Primeval Forest* (1922), *More from the Primeval Forest* (1931), and *From My African Notebook* (1938).

Reverence for life was the concept that inspired all of Schweitzer's work and prompted him to write in 1957 and 1958, urging the major nations to renounce the testing of nuclear weapons.

Schweitzer died at Lambaréné on September 4, 1965. At ninety he was still working with great vigor on his monumental three-volume *Philosophy of Civilization.*

Other Titles in the ValueTale Series